Día De Muertos

words&pictures

© 2025 Quarto Publishing Group USA Inc.
Illustrations © Alejandra Ruiz 2025
Text by Jaquelina Díaz de León Rodríguez (artist name Jaque Jours)

First published in 2025 by words & pictures,
an imprint of The Quarto Group.
100 Cummings Center, Suite 265D,
Beverly, MA 01915, USA.
T (978) 282-9590 F (978) 283-2742
www.quarto.com

EEA Representation, WTS Tax d.o.o., Žanova ulica 3, 4000 Kranj, Slovenia.

Project Editor: Anna Brett
Senior Commissioning Editor: Catharine Robertson
Designer: Clare Barber
Senior Designer: Mike Henson
Creative Director: Malena Stojić
Associate Publisher: Holly Willsher
Production Manager: Nikki Ingram

ISBN: 978-1-83600-091-4

9 8 7 6 5 4 3 2 1

Manufactured in Guangdong, China TT052025

FSC
www.fsc.org
MIX
Paper | Supporting
responsible forestry
FSC® C016973

Día De Muertos

Jaque Jours

illustrated by
Alejandra Ruiz

It's nearly Día de Muertos,
my favorite time of year!

My name is Poncho, and this is my mom,
dad, older sister, and our family dog
Bonsái. He is a tiny chihuahua!

4

Día de Muertos is the day when people we love, but who we can't hug anymore, visit us. That's why it's called "the day of the dead."

I know it might sound scary, but it's not at all! Trust me, I'm not that brave.

We have lots to do to prepare!

Every year for Día de Muertos, my family and I set up an *ofrenda* to help our loved ones find their way back home. An ofrenda is an altar used to honor those who have died. Since my grandma Luz María and my *abuelo* Rubén are no longer with us, we will place their pictures and favorite items on the altar.

This is the first year my abuelo Rubén will join the altar. He passed away two months ago. Losing someone hurts very much, but Día de Muertos makes us feel closer to them. It is a way to celebrate them.

We always build the altar in the hall near the entrance to our house, so that whoever passes by can see it from outside.

There's a lot to get ready before we can build the ofrenda! While Dad cleans the house, my older sister goes to buy all the things we will need.

She's got a long list of things to get, including candles, *cempasúchil* flowers, incense, and fruit.

Since it is the first year that we will add my abuelo Rubén to the *altar de muertos*, I am in charge of gathering some of the things he loved and used. And, of course, a good picture of him!

Mom has dusted off some old photo albums so I can look through them for photos of my grandfather. There are some photos from when my mother was a little kid! It's so cool to see what my abuelo Rubén looked like before I was born.

My sister has arrived home with cempasúchil flowers. I love the smell of them so much! We will use them to decorate the ofrenda and trace a path from the entrance of the house to the altar.

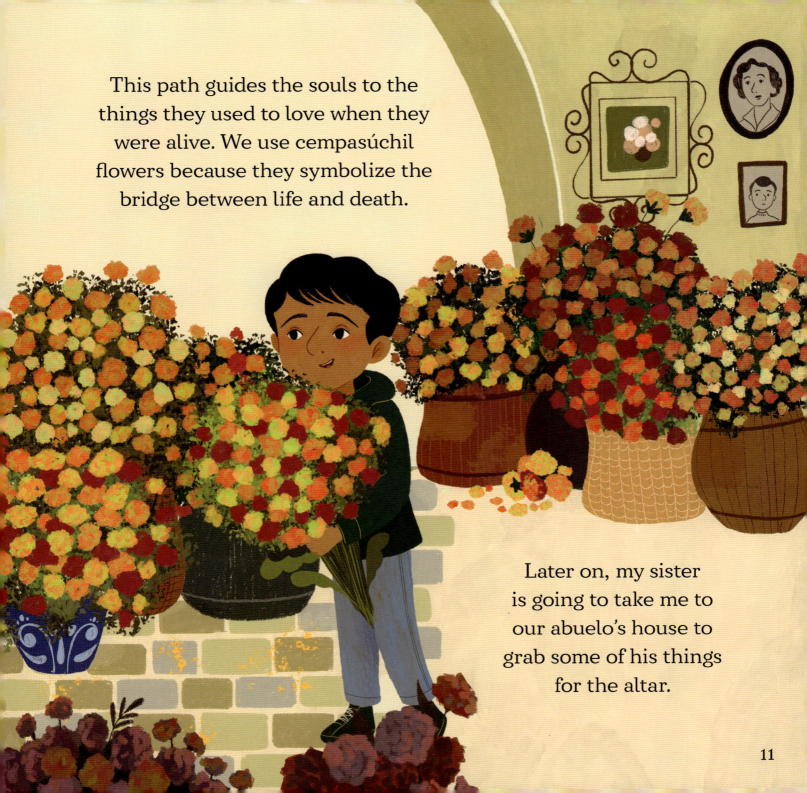

This path guides the souls to the things they used to love when they were alive. We use cempasúchil flowers because they symbolize the bridge between life and death.

Later on, my sister is going to take me to our abuelo's house to grab some of his things for the altar.

When we get to abuelo Rubén's house, I run straight to the place where he used to sit for hours and tell us amazing stories.

Seeing my grandfather's things makes me smile and remember everything we enjoyed doing together.

Abuelo Rubén loved to collect unusual things. So, I'm going to take one of the rare clay cups from his collection.

Now I need to locate his cowboy hat, his cherished brown belt, and his trusty *morral*— the small bag that he always carried to the market.

These items immediately come to mind when I think of him, so they're essential for the ofrenda!

I'm sure he will love the things I have chosen for him.

When we get home, my cousin Gustavo arrives with cardboard boxes to make the levels of the altar. These represent the three spiritual levels: Earth, Purgatory, and Heaven.

We cut, glue, and arrange the cardboard boxes to create the three levels. Then we put a tablecloth on top.

More cousins arrive!
Although they have their own
ofrenda for our grandpa, we
like to help each other.

Each family makes an ofrenda
in their own house, which
means our departed family
members always have a lot of
altars to visit every year.

The next day, my mom, sister, and I make some *papel picado*, the tissue paper decorations we display for Día de Muertos. We make them as colorful as possible!

16

They're really fun to make, although it can be challenging—the patterns are very detailed! I cut out some skull figures and my sister cuts a flower pattern. My sister is very skilled at it—I don't know how she does it! But she says she will teach me when I am older.

Día de Muertos is tomorrow, and we have lots left to do!

Now that we have gathered all the things we need, it's time to finish the ofrenda. We all work together to make it really special.

My cousin Ana helps us decorate each level of the altar with papel picado. She says it symbolizes the air. And since we have some extra decorations, she hangs some on the door and windows as well. They look so beautiful!

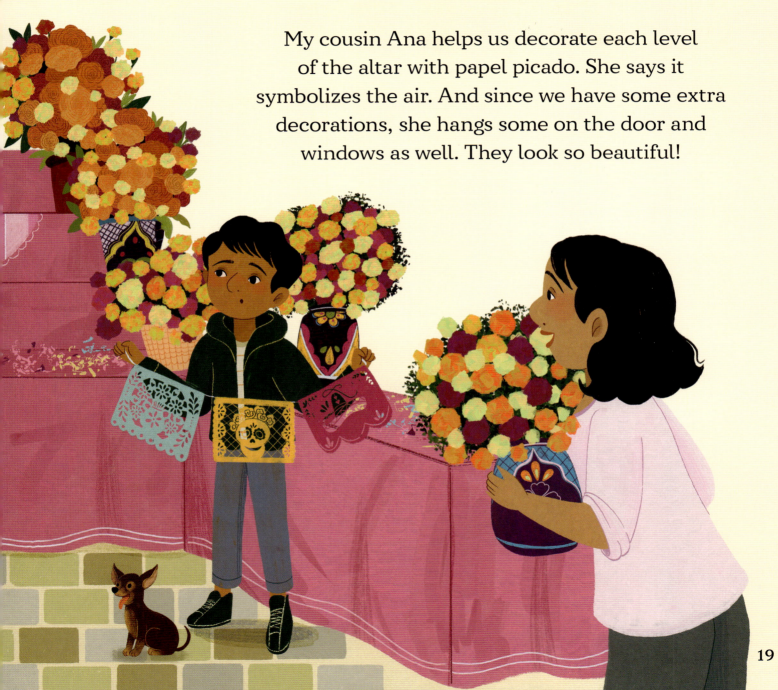

Next, my sister lays out the path of cempasúchil flowers and places candles all around to make sure our relatives see it. Maybe one or two by the window, too. There's never enough! The house looks very pretty and orange at this time of the year.

Dad places a glass of water on the altar in case the souls arrive thirsty from their long journey, and a plate of salt for the purification of the soul. The salt is also a form of protection so the souls can come again the following year.

Finally, my cousin and I place the photos and belongings of our abuelo Rubén in the remaining spaces on the altar.

It's finally Día de Muertos! My other grandma has arrived to spend the day with us. She usually helps with the food— we prepare the visiting souls' favorite traditional dishes and place them on the altar. But we also enjoy them ourselves!

My sister loves tamales and Mom loves pozole, so we all cook what we like and share some of the offerings together.

I choose to put a plate of enchiladas on the altar—they're my favorite. My grandma and I also lay out some sweet treats: the *calaveritas de azúcar* and *pan de muerto*! I always eat one of each but keep the rest for the ofrenda.

To be honest, it's impossible to make an altar without tasting all the treats that are put out for the souls.

Finally, my sister and I lay fruits on the altar. The fruits we choose all have meanings and are the offering provided by nature. Dad passes us tangerines, *guayabas*, and jicama to put in place.

They are all delicious! But the tangerines are the best—they represent sunlight. Some people say that orange is the only color the souls can see on their return. Maybe that's why we use cempasúchil flowers, too!

There's nothing like seeing the ofrenda fully assembled with all the special items of the people we miss. It looks so beautiful! I'm sure our departed family members will easily find their way home.

It's time for a well-deserved break! My family
all gather around the table to enjoy pan de muerto
with hot chocolate while we share stories about
our departed loved ones.

For my family, Día de Muertos
is all about the joy we find in
sharing stories and memories
of those who have passed away.

We look through old photographs, admire the altar, and share smiles and hugs. My mom reminds me that our time together strengthens the bonds that connect us as a family, and keeps us close to the loved ones we miss.

For Día de Muertos, many schools hold writing contests where students create literary *calaveritas*. These are poems that humorously tell a story about death! The main character can be a loved one, someone famous, or even yourself.

Writing calaveritas is one of my favorite seasonal activities! I wrote a calaverita about my abuelo Rubén for my school contest.

Before heading out to explore the town to see the other altars and decorations, I share my calaverita with my family while we eat dinner.

Everyone thinks I'll win the school contest! My abuelo Rubén brings out the best in me.

At last, we go out to greet the neighbors and admire their altars. I love seeing the street come alive with candles and flowers. There are people dressed as Catrinas—female skulls with colorful dresses and flowers in their hair—and their counterparts, los Catrínes—skulls in dapper suits and hats.

We move closer to the town center as the parade begins. The crowd is huge! Dad lifts me onto his shoulders so I can get a better view of the skulls—some of them are enormous! I love the music. Everyone is dancing and having fun.

Día de Muertos is truly the best celebration of the year!

Although it's difficult to lose someone you love, celebrating Día de Muertos is comforting as it allows us to feel their presence every year. It reminds us that they live on in our memories, making it feel as though they never truly left.

Death is part of life's journey. That doesn't mean losing someone doesn't hurt. But each year, at the start of November, we have the opportunity to open the bridge for souls to return to the world of the living and feel our relatives close again.

I can't wait to make next year's ofrenda and welcome them again!

33

What is Día de Muertos?

Día de Muertos is one of the most significant celebrations in Mexico. It is a fun and colorful festival centered around setting up altars, or ofrendas, dedicated to those who have passed away.

Altars range from a simple candle and photo on a nightstand, to decorating an entire room. However, they all share the same purpose: to honor those who have departed and to help them find their way back home to visit their families.

In Mexico, many people don't see death as something to be scared of, or as the definitive end of life. Instead, death is thought of as going to another place we can't see.

HISTORY

Día de Muertos is celebrated on November 1 and 2, but some people begin preparations a month in advance.

The tradition of celebrating Día de Muertos originated over 700 years ago with Indigenous peoples, primarily the Mexica (Aztec) and other Mesoamerican cultures. The Mexica honored their ancestors, and had rituals involving offerings to the deceased.

Incense was often burnt as a sacred offering to the deceased.

When Spanish invaders arrived in Mexico in the early 16th century, they brought a Catholic tradition called Día de los Fieles Difuntos (All Souls' Day), which is celebrated on November 2. All Souls' Day honors people who have passed away and focuses on praying for those who need extra help to reach heaven.

Today, Día de Muertos blends Indigenous traditions with Christian elements, creating a distinctive celebration that honors the departed while also celebrating life.

It's important to learn about our history.

DÍA DE MUERTOS AND HALLOWEEN

People often think that Día de Muertos and Halloween are connected because they both happen around the same time, and this closeness has made them blend a bit with each other. Some Mexicans now like to dress up as La Catrina for Halloween as well. But the two celebrations come from different cultural and historical backgrounds and serve distinct purposes. Día de Muertos focuses on honoring deceased loved ones, while Halloween centers around spooky and playful elements.

Día de Muertos Celebrations Around Mexico

People dress up as La Catrina and El Catrín at a parade in Mexico City.

Día de Muertos is celebrated differently across the regions of Mexico, depending on the area's location, culture, and heritage.

OAXACA is renowned for its elaborate Día de Muertos festivities, including the vibrant *muerteadas*, parades that blend dance, live music, theater, and carnival. These celebrations can take place in homes, community spaces, or even cemeteries. Participants often wear colorful costumes, like skeletons or masks inspired by Oaxacan folklore, coming together to share stories about their deceased loved ones.

MEXICO CITY is famous for its grand Día de Muertos parade, which includes decorated floats, intricate costumes, and live music. Large altars, known as Mega Ofrendas, are set up in public spaces around the city. Cempasúchil flowers also line Paseo de la Reforma, one of the city's busiest avenues.

PÁTZCUARO is a city on the edge of Lake Pátzcuaro, and Janitzio is an island in the lake. On the night of November 1, people sail in small, candlelit boats from Pátzcuaro to the island. Families then spend the night gathered in cemeteries, surrounding the graves with flowers, candles, and food.

In **SAN LUIS POTOSÍ**, people celebrate a unique variation of Día de Muertos known as Xantolo, which reflects the customs and cultural identity of the local Huastec Indigenous peoples. Participants wear elaborate masks and costumes representing mythical characters, and the festivities also include rituals like the Dance of the Machetes, where dancers perform using decorated machetes.

In Guerrero, particularly in **TAXCO**, the celebration incorporates Indigenous Mixtec and Nahua traditions. Altars may feature papier-mâché figures representing deities from these cultures, and costumes of mythical figures like the maize god. The celebrations blend local customs with elements from Mexico's ancient civilizations.

Families lay candles and flowers around the graves of their ancestors in Pátzcuaro.

Traditional masks are worn during celebrations in Taxco.

Día de Muertos Symbols

The tradition of Día de Muertos is passed down the generations through practices, objects, and symbols that reflect Mexico's identity and culture.

LA CATRINA

La Catrina is one of the most important symbols of Día de Muertos. In 1910, illustrator José Guadalupe Posada created this female skull character to criticize Mexican high society and its obsession with adopting European fashion instead of embracing Indigenous roots. Muralist Diego Rivera later named her La Catrina when he included her in his mural *Sueño de una Tarde Dominical en la Alameda Central* (Dream of a Sunday Afternoon in Alameda Central). Since then, it has been widely adopted in Día de Muertos celebrations.

CALAVERITAS DE AZÚCAR

Calaveritas de azúcar (sugar skulls) are a crucial element of an ofrenda. The Mexica (Aztecs) used to make figures with amaranth and honey as offerings to their gods, and this slowly became part of the Día de Muertos altar tradition. These sugar skulls are decorated with bright colors and details, symbolizing that beauty can also be found after death. They are made of sugar and their sweetness is believed to help lighten the journey of the departed.

PAN DE MUERTO

Pan de muerto is an essential part of an ofrenda and a staple during this time of year in Mexico. It is often enjoyed in October and November with a cup of hot chocolate. On the ofrenda, it is included as nourishment for the visiting souls. Its circular shape symbolizes the cycle of life and death.

CEMPASÚCHIL FLOWERS

Cempasúchil flowers are one of the most iconic elements of an ofrenda during Día de Muertos. The name comes from the Náhuatl word *cempohualxochitl*, which means "twenty flowers," as each blossom appears to be made up of many smaller flowers clustered together. The flower's bright orange color and strong scent are believed to help guide the souls back to Earth during Día de Muertos.

CANDLES

Candles also play an important role on the Día de Muertos altar. Candles light the way for the departed souls, guiding them back to the world of the living. Each candle can have special meaning, symbolizing different aspects of life and death.

Make Your Own Pan de Muerto!

Pan de muerto is one of the most popular foods enjoyed during Día de Muertos. Its name means "bread of the dead." With the help of an adult, you can make your own sweet and delicious pan de muerto to enjoy. Here's what you'll need:

INGREDIENTS

- ½ cup milk
- 1 ½ tablespoons instant dry yeast
- 3 ⅔ cups all-purpose flour
- ¾ cup sugar
- 3 eggs
- 1 teaspoon orange blossom water
- 1 tablespoon orange zest
- 1 teaspoon salt
- ½ cup butter at room temperature
- Additional sugar, butter, oil, and flour

DIRECTIONS

1. Pour the milk (make sure it's not too hot or too cold) into a medium bowl. Add the yeast, 1 tablespoon of all-purpose flour, and 1 tablespoon of sugar. Stir well until fully combined. Let it rest until it doubles in size, which should take about 10 minutes.

2. Put the rest of the flour on your countertop in the shape of a volcano, with a hole in the center.

3. In the center of the flour volcano place the yeast mixture, remaining sugar, eggs, orange blossom water, and the orange zest. Sprinkle the salt around the edge.

4. Mix the ingredients. Start by stirring the center, then gradually bring the flour from the edges into the center. Once the dough is combined, add the butter on top. Mix thoroughly until the dough becomes sticky.

5. Knead the mixture until smooth and elastic (can take 20 minutes). If it's sticking, sprinkle a little flour on your countertop, but don't use too much as the dough should remain soft and smooth.

6. Take a bowl and lightly coat the inside with oil using your hands. With the remaining oil on your hands, shape the dough into a ball and place it in the bowl. Cover the bowl with plastic wrap and let the dough rise until it doubles in size. This may take about 1.5 hours.

7. Line a baking sheet with parchment paper. Lightly flour your countertop, then turn the bowl upside down to release the dough. Flatten and roll it out. Divide it into four equal parts. Set aside one part. Cut the remaining pieces in half again, shape them into six balls, and place them on the baking sheet, leaving space between each ball. You can use a second baking sheet if necessary.

8. Sprinkle a little flour on the remaining dough and shape it into a long roll. Divide it into four pieces, saving one for later. Cut the other three into 12 small pieces.

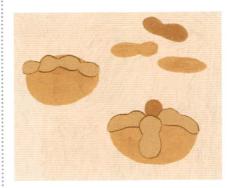

9. Using three fingers, roll each piece to form long, skinny bone shapes. Place two across the top of each of the larger dough balls to form an X shape.

10. Make six small balls with the remaining dough and put them in the center for decoration.

11. Lightly cover the baking sheet with plastic wrap and let the dough rise until it puffs up further, which should take about 1 hour.

12. With an adult's help, preheat the oven to 350°F (175°C). Then bake the pan de muerto for 20 minutes until golden brown. Carefully remove from the oven and let them cool for 15 minutes.

13. For the best and final touch, brush the bread with melted butter and sprinkle with sugar! Enjoy!

Make Your Own Papel Picado

Papel picado is made with vibrant colors and detailed patterns. It symbolizes the fragility of life, and is used to decorate ofrendas, houses, tombs, streets, and even parties. You can hang it up wherever you like, making everything look very colorful! If you want to make your own designs, here's how.

My sister created these amazing designs!

YOU WILL NEED

- Tissue paper in different colors (approximately 12 x 9 inches)
- Marker pen
- Scissors
- Tape
- Yarn (or string)

DIRECTIONS

1. Stack a few sheets of tissue paper together. This makes it easier to cut multiple layers at once. You can use one color or mix different colors.

2. Fold the stack of tissue paper in half lengthwise, then fold it in half again to make a smaller, thicker rectangle.

3. Fold the folded sheet in half one more time. Use a marker to put a small dot in the corner. This will help you remember where not to cut so there is enough paper left at the top.

4. Use a marker to draw simple patterns along the edges of the tissue paper. You can include elements related to Día de Muertos, such as flowers, skulls, candles, or any other shapes you like.

5. Next, cut out the patterns but avoid the area with the dot.

6. If you want to add decoration to the center of your papel picado, fold the top of your rectangle down to the bottom. Draw half of your design on this folded edge, then cut it out.

7. Gently unfold the tissue paper to reveal your papel picado design. You should have multiple layers with the same pattern.

8. Cut a piece of yarn to the length you need for hanging your papel picado. Tape the yarn to the top edge of each piece of papel picado, placing them next to each other all along the yarn.

9. Find a place to hang your papel picado, such as across a window, on a wall, or on your ofrenda! Tape or pin the ends of the yarn to the desired spot.

You can make as many designs as you want. Try folding the tissue paper in different ways before drawing and cutting out your shapes. The same design in different colors will look great too. Let your imagination run wild!

La Catrina or El Catrín

La Catrina is a fancy skeleton, known for her elegant appearance with a large, decorated hat and a vintage dress. El Catrín is the male version of La Catrina. Similar in style with a sophisticated look and always dressed in a suit.

During Día de Muertos, these figures are featured in decorations, altars, events, and parades, making the celebration colorful and fun! If you want to dress up as them, here's how you can do it.

DIRECTIONS

1. Start by putting on a white face paint base. Use a sponge or brush to cover your face evenly. Let it dry a little.

2. Use black face paint or eyeliner to draw the outlines of a skull on your face. Draw two big circles for eyes, a curved line for the nose, and a big smile with teeth.

YOU WILL NEED

- White face paint
- Makeup sponges or brushes for applying face paint
- Black eyeliner or face paint pen
- Colored face paint (black, red, blue, or other colors you like)
- Paintbrushes of different sizes
- Brightly colored clothing (dresses, suits, or any fancy outfits)
- Accessories (hats, flowers, bows, and ties)

3. Paint colorful flowers or patterns around your eyes and on your cheeks. You can use bright colors like red, pink, blue, and yellow. Let your creativity shine!

4. Use a fine brush or face paint pen to add small details to your skull, like cracks, swirls, or dots around the flowers. You can also add flowers, hearts, or even spiderwebs.

5. Finally, get dressed!

For **La Catrina**: Wear a colorful, flowy dress. Decorate a large hat with fake flowers, ribbons, and sequins. You can use glue to attach these decorations to the hat.

For **El Catrín**: Put on a suit or a smart shirt with a tie. Add a stylish top hat and attach a flower to your jacket with a safety pin or glue.

Now you're ready to celebrate as **La Catrina** or **El Catrín**! Enjoy the festivities and embrace the spirit of Día de Muertos.

Quiz

Let's see how much you remember about Día de Muertos!

1. When does Día de Muertos take place?
a. October 31
b. November 1 and 2
c. March 18

2. Who visits living relatives during Día de Muertos?
a. Departed loved ones, family members, or people who have died
b. Ghosts from ancient times
c. People from other countries

3. Why do people set up altars, or ofrendas, for Día de Muertos?
a. To decorate their homes
b. To honor their deceased family or ancestors
c. To teach children about their heritage

4. What is the name of the orange flowers used to decorate ofrendas?
a. Cempasúchil flowers
b. Pumpkin flowers
c. Margarita flowers

5. Where are ofrendas often set up?
a. Inside a bedroom
b. A public square
c. Near a home's entrance so passersby can see it from outside

6. What is the name of the female skull people like to dress as for Día de Muertos?
a. La Catrina
b. La Llorona
c. La Chilindrina

7. What is the name of the sweet bread eaten during Día de Muertos?
a. Pan dulce
b. Pan de muerto
c. Conchita

8. What are the colorful paper cutouts often used to decorate ofrendas called?

a. Papel de muerto

b. Papel picado

c. Papel maché

9. What kinds of candies are commonly made in the shape of skulls for Día de Muertos?

a. Skull lollipops

b. Chocolate skulls

c. Sugar skulls

10. What do people light on the ofrendas to help guide the spirits home?

a. Candles

b. A nearby fireplace

c. Incense

Answers on the next page!

Answers

1. **b** – November 1 and 2
2. **a** – Departed loved ones, family members, or people who have died
3. **b** – To honor their deceased family or ancestors
4. **a** – Cempasúchil flowers
5. **c** – Near a home's entrance so passersby can see it from outside
6. **a** – La Catrina
7. **b** – Pan de muerto
8. **b** – Papel picado
9. **c** – Sugar skulls (calaveritas de azúcar)
10. **a** – Candles